23/2/09

A CHILD'S BOOK OF ART

DISCOVER GREAT PAINTINGS

Lucy Micklethwait

www.dk.com

For Janey and Welly

Senior Editor Jane Baldock
Designer Veneta Altham
Managing Editor Sarah Phillips
Managing Art Editor Peter Bailey
DTP Designers Greg Bryant and Sarah Williams
Jacket Designer Joe Hoyle
Production Josie Alabaster
Picture Researchers Jo Walton and Katherine Mesquita

Published in Great Britain
by Dorling Kindersley Limited,

ISBN: 0-7513-5501-1

Colour reproduction by GRB, Italy
Printed and bound in Italy by L.E.G.O.

Picture Credits
The publisher would like to thank the following for their kind permission to reproduce the photographs:
t = top, c = centre, r = right, l = left, a = above, b = below,

Alte Pinakothek, Munich/Artothek: *Portrait of the Marquise de Pompadour* 3br, 16/17, 30cla;
Galleria degli Uffizi/AKG London/ Erich Lessing: *Primavera (Spring)* 6/7, 30cra, 31c;
© David Hockney: *Self-Portrait with Blue Guitar* 3tl, 28/29, 30clb, 31br;
Kunsthistorisches Museum, Vienna/AKG London/Erich Lessing: *Hunters in the Snow (Winter)*, 2br, 10/11, 30cb, 31bl;
Musée d'Orsay, Paris: *The Bedroom at Arles* 3bl, 24/25, 30bl; **Courtesy, Museum of Fine Arts, Boston:** *The Fog Warning* Otis Norcross Fund, 22/23, 30tr;
National Gallery, London: *The Ambassadors* 8/9, 30tc;
National Galleries of Scotland: *An Old Woman Cooking Eggs* 12/13, 30cl;
© 1998 Board of Trustees National Gallery of Art, Washington: *Saint George and the Dragon*, Ailsa Mellon Bruce Fund, 4/5, 30tl; *The Dancing Couple*, Widener Collection 14/15, 30br, *Tropical Forest with Monkeys*, John Hay Whitney Collection, 3cr, 26/27, 30bcr;
© Tate Gallery, London 1998: *The Death of Major Peirson* 18/19, 30cr, 31tr; *Christ in the Carpenter's Shop* 20/21, 30bl.

Jacket:
Alte Pinakothek, Munich/Artothek: *Portrait of the Marquise de Pompadour* Back Jacket br;
© David Hockney: *Self-Portrait with Blue Guitar* (detail), Back Jacket cr;
National Gallery, London: *The Ambassadors* Back Jacket tr;
National Galleries of Scotland: *An Old Woman Cooking Eggs* Back Jacket tc;
© 1998 Board of Trustees National Gallery of Art, Washington: *Baby at Play* 1876 Thomas Eakins, John Hay Whitney Collection, Front Jacket tl (inset); *Tropical Forest with Monkeys* John Hay Whitney Collection, Front Jacket, *Saint George and the Dragon* Ailsa Mellon Bruce Fund, Back Jacket bl; *The Dancing Couple* Widener Collection, Back Jacket cb.

Contents

Become an Art Detective and Discover Great Paintings

Every painting is like a mystery waiting to be solved. To find out what is going on, look at the evidence and ask yourself questions about it. What are the people wearing? What is the weather like? Is it a noisy scene? Is it sad, happy, or frightening? Look at shapes, colours, and textures. Try to work out the age of the painting and identify unfamiliar objects.

Only the artist has all the answers to all the riddles in a picture, so you can have fun looking for clues and drawing your own conclusions. You may make some interesting discoveries.

In this book we have made the investigation easier for you. On the left-hand page there are questions, and on the right-hand page there are facts about the picture and many of the answers. We have added a few details about the artist and indicated the size of the real painting by showing it in relation to an average 5-year-old child.

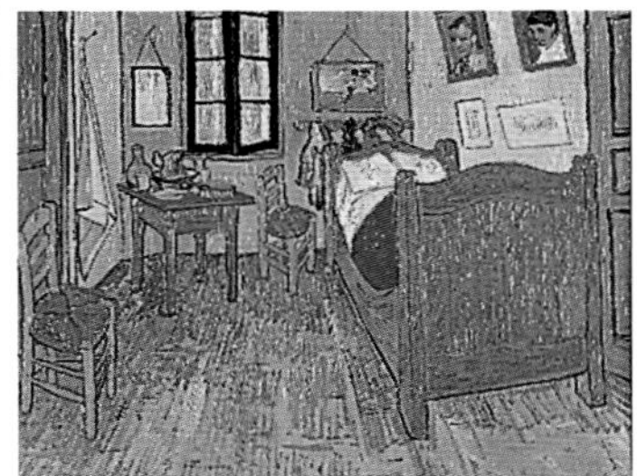

Once you have mastered the simple art of looking and asking questions, you can apply your art detective skills to any painting in the world.

Lucy Micklethwait

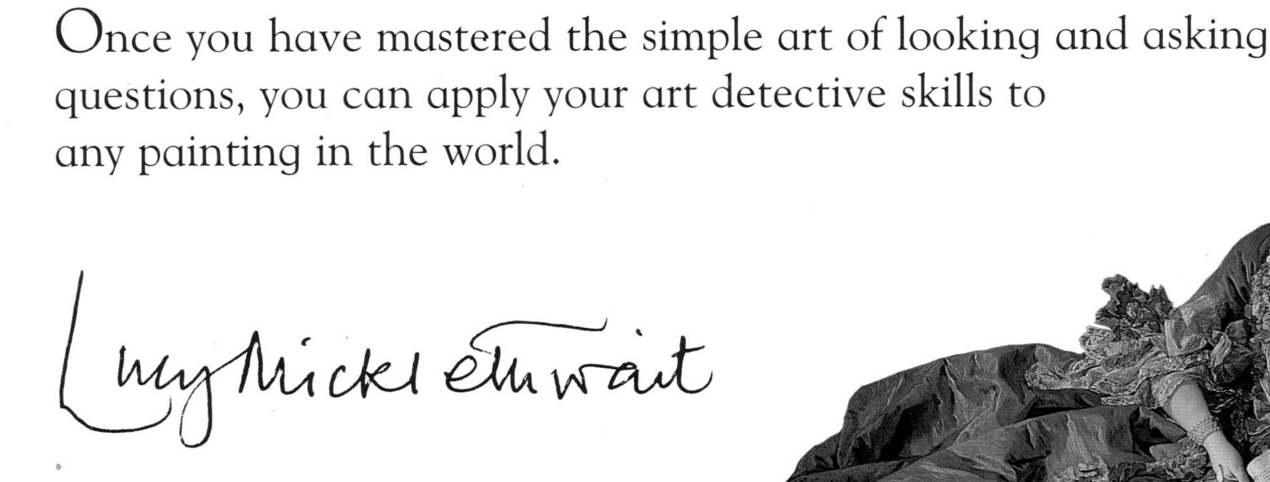

Saint George and the Dragon

Long ago in a country now forgotten, a wicked dragon lived in a lake near a king's castle. Each day the dragon ate one sheep. When there were no more sheep in the countryside, he started eating the people from the town. Soon it was the turn of the king's daughter. When she saw the dragon, she knelt down and prayed. Just then Saint George appeared. Look at the picture and find out what happened next.

The investigation

What do you think the dragon stands for?

What is the princess doing? Describe what she is wearing.

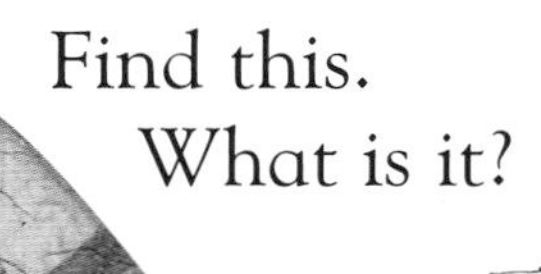

Find this. What is it?

What can you see reflected in the calm water?

Do you think that the artist used fine paintbrushes or thick paintbrushes?

What is Saint George doing? Describe what he is wearing.

Who do you think lives here?

Who has been eating this?

The facts

Look closer

If you look closely you can see two horsemen riding towards the king's castle.

This is the king's castle. He lives here with the princess.

The town is reflected in the water.

The princess is praying to be saved.

These fine lines tell us that the artist used very fine paintbrushes. He probably used a magnifying glass to help him see what he was doing.

This skull, and the human skull below the dragon, show that the dragon has been eating animals and people.

Saint George was made patron saint of England. The red cross on his shield appears on the English flag.

He wears spurs on his feet to make his horse go faster.

He is using a lance to kill the dragon.

The dragon is a symbol that stands for evil.

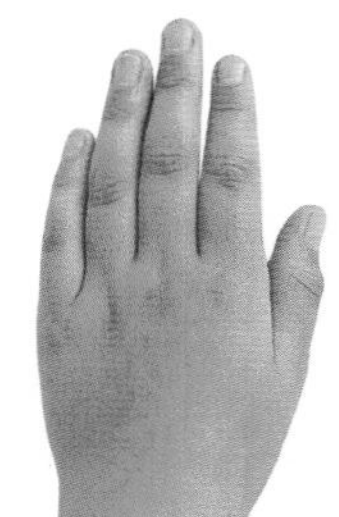

Behind the scenes

Van der Weyden used oil paint on a small piece of wood about the size of your hand. He painted the picture between about 1432 and 1435, so it is the oldest in the book.

ARTIST Rogier van der Weyden

- He was born in about 1400 and died in 1464.
- He had a busy workshop in Brussels with many assistants and pupils.
- His name means Roger of the Meadow.

Primavera (Spring)

The ancient Greeks and Romans believed that there were a great many gods and goddesses who looked after life on earth. Venus was the goddess of love. She was beautiful. Here she is in a garden with some companions. Look closely at the picture and find out who's who in the garden.

Find the blue man with wings.

The investigation

Can you find these hands?

What do you think Mercury is doing with this?

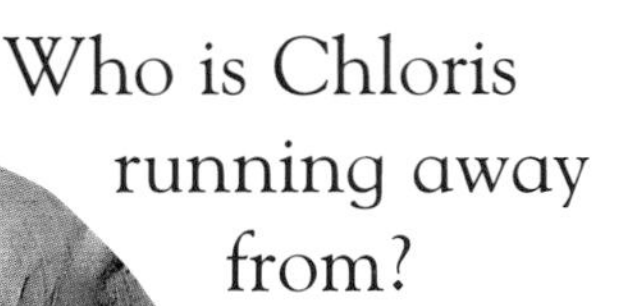

Who is Chloris running away from?

Find this little boy. What is he doing?

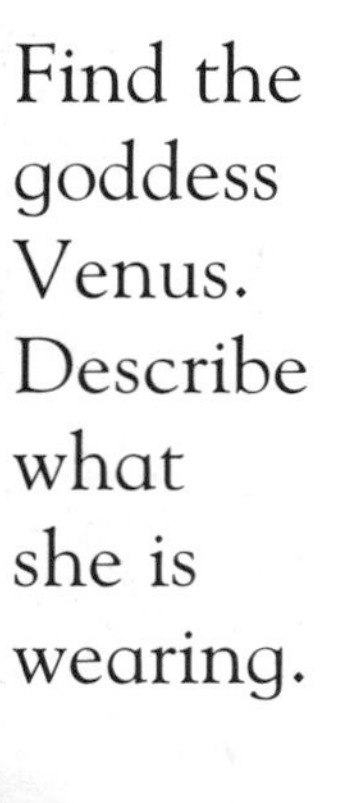

Find the goddess Venus. Describe what she is wearing.

This is Flora. What is she doing?

Can you find these feet? What is unusual about the boots?

facts

Look closer

Cupid, the god of love, often stirs up trouble. If he fires a golden arrow at someone, they fall in love, but if he fires an arrow made of lead, they start to argue. He is aiming a golden arrow at one of the Three Graces. He is wearing a blindfold.

Mercury has a magic stick with snakes on it. He is using it to push the clouds out of the garden.

Venus, the goddess of love

Cupid, the son of Venus

Fruit trees

Zephyr, the west wind of spring

Mercury is the messenger of the gods. The wings on his boots help him to fly fast.

The Three Graces are dancing. They are Venus' attendants.

Flora, the goddess of flowers, is scattering flowers on the ground.

This is Chloris. When she married Zephyr, flowers spilled out of her mouth and she turned into Flora. So Chloris and Flora are the same person.

Behind the scenes

Botticelli used tempera (powdered colours mixed with egg) on a huge panel made of wood. He painted the picture in about 1480.

ARTIST Sandro Botticelli

- He was born in Florence in about 1445. He died in 1510.
- He painted many pictures for the Medici family, rulers of Florence.
- His real name was Alessandro Di Mariano Filipepi.

The Dancing Couple

It's party time. Everyone is invited, young and old. Musicians are playing. The guests are eating, drinking, and chatting, and someone has started to dance. Imagine that you are one of the guests at the party and find out a little about life in Holland three hundred years ago.

The investigation

What do you think this lady is thinking?

Find this man. Describe his clothes.

? What noises would you be able to hear if you were at this party?

Find out why the stem of this pipe is so long.

This boy is playing a violin. What other musical instrument can you see?

Find this boy. What is he doing?

What do you think is in this jug?

? Find the artist's signature.

The artist is somewhere in the picture. Can you find him?

The facts

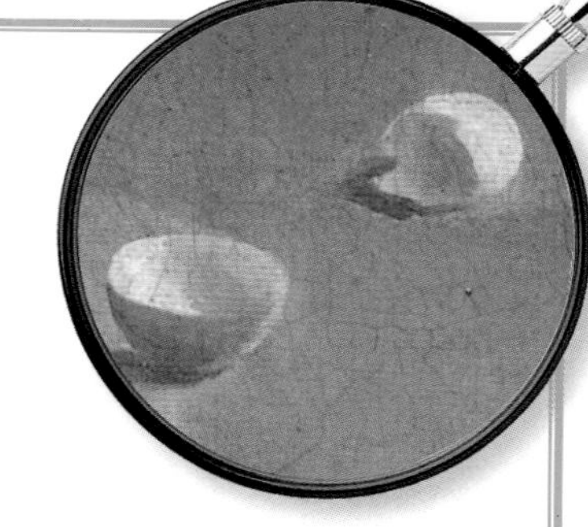

Look closer

The eggshells, dying flowers, and bubbles are symbols. They tell us that life is short and that good things, like parties, never last long.

The artist

The elderly people are watching the dancing.

A birdcage

The artist may be suggesting that it is better to be in church than at a party.

A violin

A flute

A jug of wine

The artist's signature

Both young boys and girls wore dresses. This child is holding a wooden toy and is wearing a padded hat for protection.

The stem of the pipe is long so that the smoke can cool down before reaching the mouth. The terracotta bowl is filled with hot coals for lighting the pipe.

This boy is blowing bubbles.

Behind the scenes

Steen put the date of this painting, 1663, beside his signature. He used oil paint on canvas.

ARTIST Jan Steen

- He was born in Holland in about 1626 and died in 1679.
- He is famous for his cheerful scenes of everyday life in Holland. Often they contain hidden messages.
- If someone describes your home as a "Jan Steen household" it means that they think it is untidy.

The Death of Major Peirson

It is a cold January morning in 1781. We are in Jersey, an island off the coast of France. Jersey belongs to Britain but the French want it back. The French army has landed in the dead of night, marched to St. Helier (the capital), and forced the governor to surrender. The British soldiers, led by Major Francis Peirson, have launched a counter-attack and there is a fierce battle in the town centre. Find out what happens.

Who is this? What is he doing?

The investigation

? Imagine you are watching this battle from one of the windows. Describe the noises you would hear.

Which side does this flag belong to?

? Do you think this battle really did take place, or did the artist make it up?

Who is this? What has happened to him?

What do the soldiers have attached to the ends of their guns?

Who is this wounded man?

? Describe the uniform of the British soldiers.

Find the drummer.

The facts

Look closer

The gold statue is of King George II of England. It still stands in the Royal Square in the centre of St. Helier.

There are more British soldiers on the hill.

The soldiers are carrying rifles with bayonets.

The Union Jack is the British flag. The British won the battle.

The French sniper who shot the Major is wounded. The French soldiers have cockades (rosettes) on their hats.

Pompey is Major Peirson's servant. He is shooting at the French sniper who shot his master.

Major Peirson has been shot by a French sniper and he is dying. He is only 23 years old.

The officers are carrying swords.

The women and children are terrified.

Behind the scenes

Copley was asked to record this scene shortly after the battle took place on 6 January 1781. He finished it in 1783. He used oil paint on a huge canvas.

ARTIST
John Singleton Copley

- This American painter was born in 1738 and died in 1815.
- He taught himself to paint.
- He left his home in Boston in 1774 and settled in London.

Christ in the Carpenter's Shop

The Bible tells us that Jesus Christ was the son of Mary who was married to a carpenter called Joseph. They lived 2000 years ago. Here is Jesus in Joseph's workshop. Find out who is with him and what has just happened.

The investigation

What machinery would you expect to see in a carpenter's shop today?

How does Joseph earn a living?

Who is this?

If Jesus were living now, what do you think he would look like?

Saint John is Jesus' cousin. What is he doing?

Who is the elderly lady?

Find these sheep.

What has Jesus done to his hand?

What is this used for?

Look closer

The dove stands for the Holy Spirit, which will be sent from heaven when Jesus is baptized. Today we use the dove as a symbol of peace.

The flock of sheep stands for Jesus' followers.

Pincers for pulling out nails

Saint Anne is the mother of Mary. She is Jesus' grandmother.

Tools are hanging on the wall. There is a bow saw for cutting curves in wood.

Joseph is wearing a carpenter's apron.

A bird is drinking from a bowl on the sill.

Timber store

A half-finished basket

The assistant is holding the planks together.

A vice for holding wood is fixed to the work bench.

Mary, mother of Jesus

Jesus has hurt his hand on a nail. Blood has dripped onto his foot. The scene reminds us that one day he will be crucified.

Saint John is bringing water to wash Jesus' hand. He is wearing an animal skin. When the boys are grown up, John will baptize Jesus with holy water in the River Jordan.

Behind the scenes

Millais painted this scene between 1849 and 1850. He used oil paint on canvas. His father modelled for Joseph's head but a real carpenter modelled for the arms.

ARTIST John Everett Millais

- An English artist, he was born in 1829 and died in 1896.
- He went to art school when he was only 11 years old.
- He was the first artist ever to be knighted. He became Sir John Everett Millais.

The Fog Warning

The fisherman is far out at sea. He has been towed to the deep water by a sailing ship and then left to get on with his work. It is a dangerous way to earn a living but today he has caught at least two fine fish. Suddenly he hears the sound of the ship's horn. He looks up at the sky and realises he is in great danger. Find out why.

The investigation

What do you think the fisherman is looking at?

Why is the sea so rough?

What do you think will happen if the fisherman does not reach the ship in time?

Are the fish in the bow or the stern of the boat?

Describe how you would feel if *you* were rowing the boat.

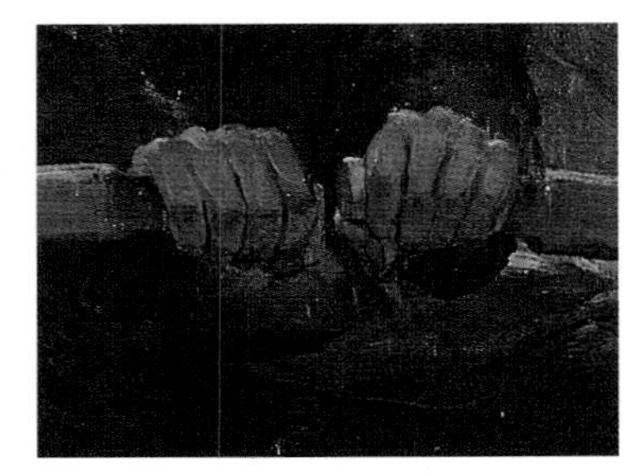

The fisherman is rowing as fast as he can. Why?

There is a strange shape in the sky. What is it?

Find out what sort of fish this is. Does it live in salt water or fresh water?

Find this. What is it?

Think of two things you can smell in the picture.

The facts

Look closer

The artist's signature is hidden in the corner of the picture.

The bow of the boat is riding high on the crest of a wave. This type of rowing boat is called a dory.

The anchor is a traditional symbol standing for hope.

A dark bank of fog is spreading across the sky.

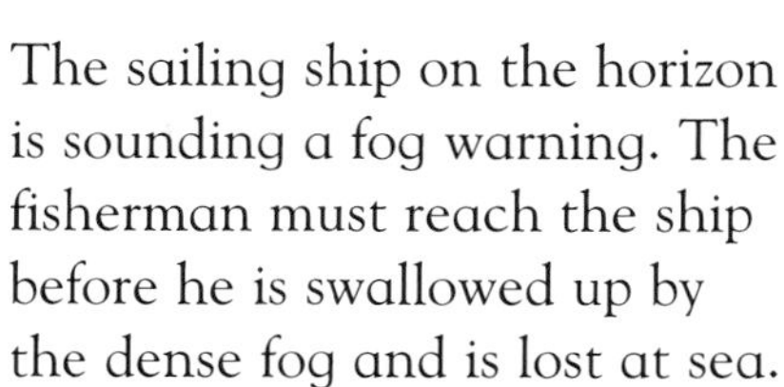

The sailing ship on the horizon is sounding a fog warning. The fisherman must reach the ship before he is swallowed up by the dense fog and is lost at sea.

The oars are held in position by wooden pegs fixed to the side of the boat.

With broad sweeping brushstrokes the artist has given a powerful impression of the stormy sea.

The barrel is used to stop a fishing net sinking. Attached to the net, it floats on the surface of the water.

The halibut are weighing down the stern of the dory.

The water is deep and dark. The wind is up and the waves are getting bigger.

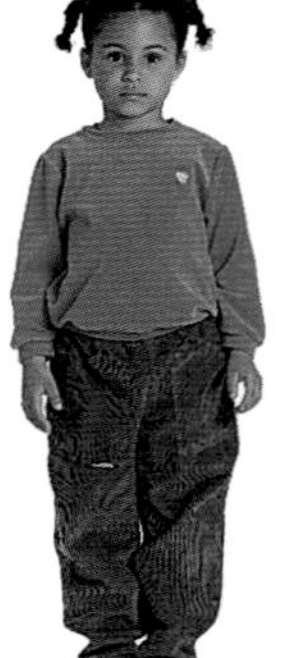

Behind the scenes

Homer was fascinated by the power of the sea and painted many dramatic seascapes. This one was painted in 1885. He used oil paint on canvas.

ARTIST Winslow Homer

- An American artist, he was born in 1836 and died in 1910.
- Before he became a painter, Homer worked as a magazine illustrator.
- He lived for much of his life in a house overlooking the Atlantic Ocean.

Tropical Forest with Monkeys

Imagine you are travelling through a tropical forest. You are hot and tired. Suddenly, you come across this scene. You hardly dare to breathe. In the clearing before you there are monkeys, lots of them. Some are quite still, while others are swinging through the branches.

Can you see this monkey? What is he doing?

The investigation

How many exotic flowers can you count in the picture?

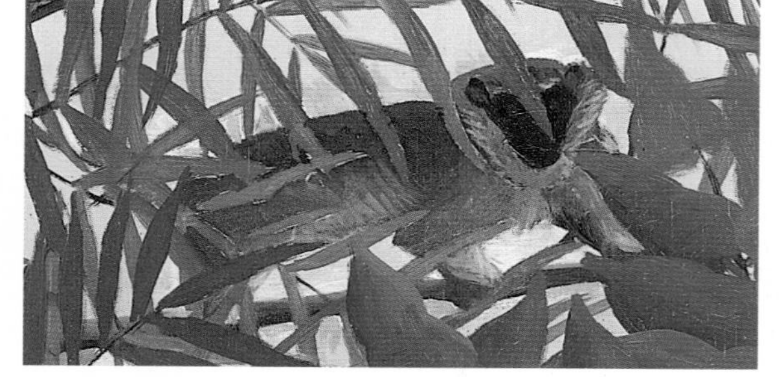

Where is this monkey hiding?

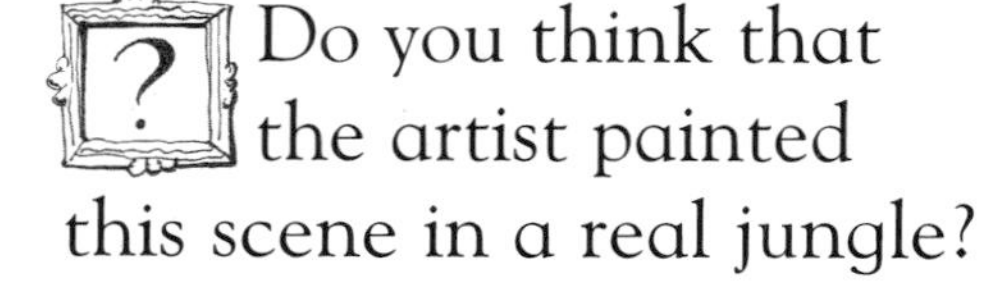

Do you think that the artist painted this scene in a real jungle?

This monkey is holding a green stick. What is it for?

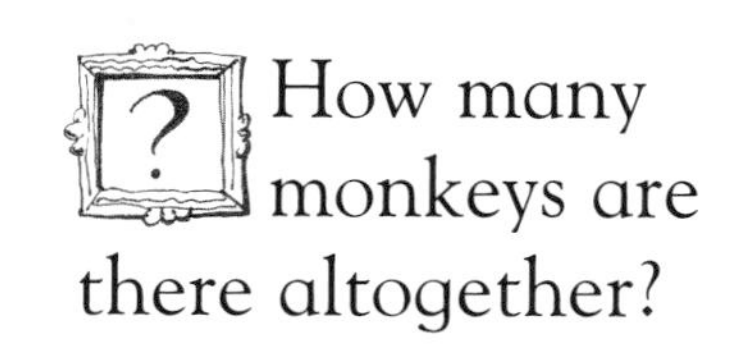

How many monkeys are there altogether?

What is this monkey doing?

Look out for danger. Find this face.

The facts

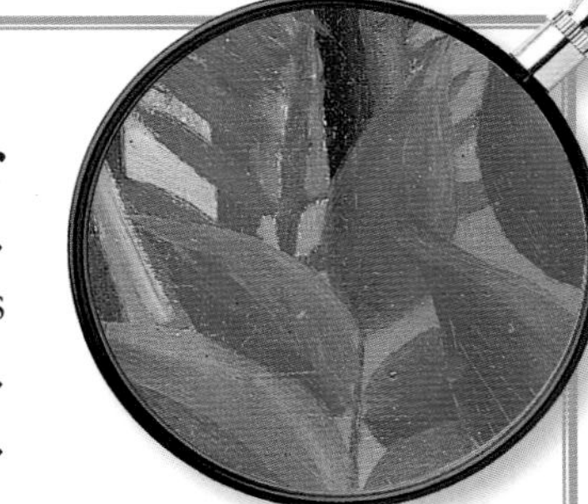

Look closer

There are lots of leaves of different shapes. The artist was inspired by the plants in the botanical gardens in Paris. He never went to a tropical forest.

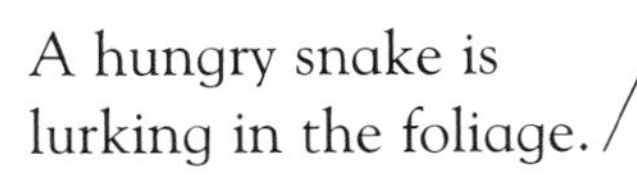

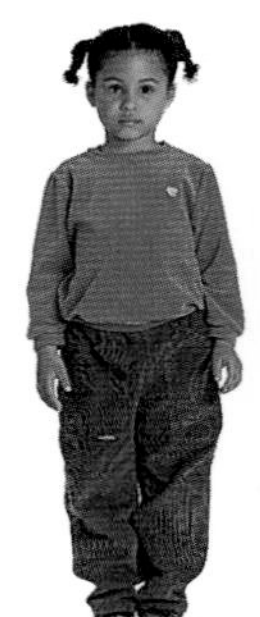

Behind the scenes

Rousseau painted 25 jungle scenes altogether. He wrote the date of this one, 1910, under his signature. He used oil paint on canvas.

ARTIST Henri Rousseau

- He was born in France in 1844 and died in 1910.
- His nickname was "Le Douanier" (customs officer) because he worked in the Paris Customs Office.
- He took up painting as a hobby.

Self-Portrait with Blue Guitar

When he painted this picture, the artist David Hockney was having fun with shapes, colours, patterns, and different styles of painting. It is a self-portrait so the man at the table is Hockney himself. He is busy drawing a picture of a blue guitar. He was inspired by a poem he had once read called "The Man with the Blue Guitar".

The investigation

What do you think this pot contains? How many pots are there altogether?

The artist is concentrating. What is he drawing?

Describe the artist and his clothes.

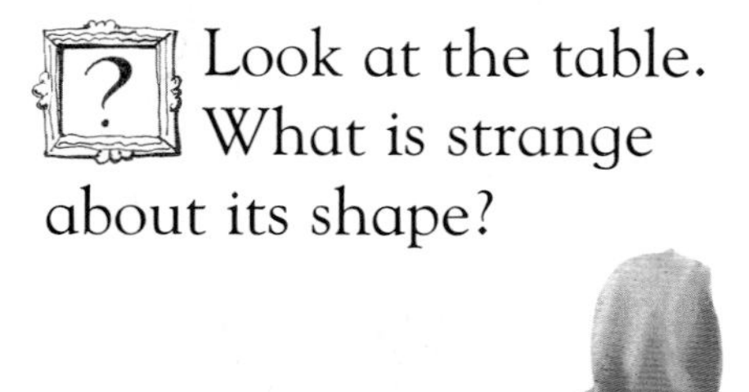

Look at the table. What is strange about its shape?

Find this.

What is odd about the dark shape under the chair?

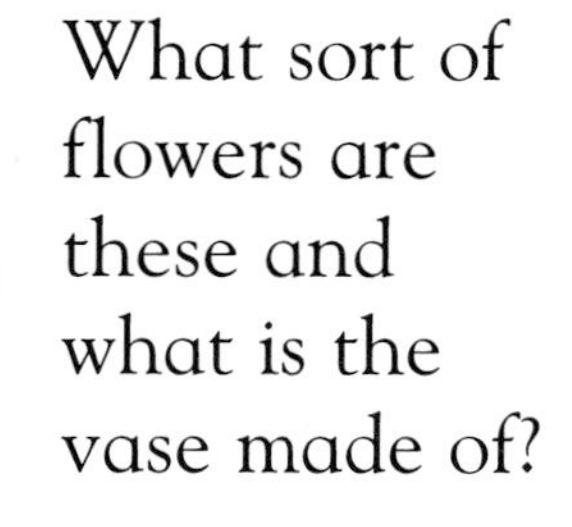

What sort of flowers are these and what is the vase made of?

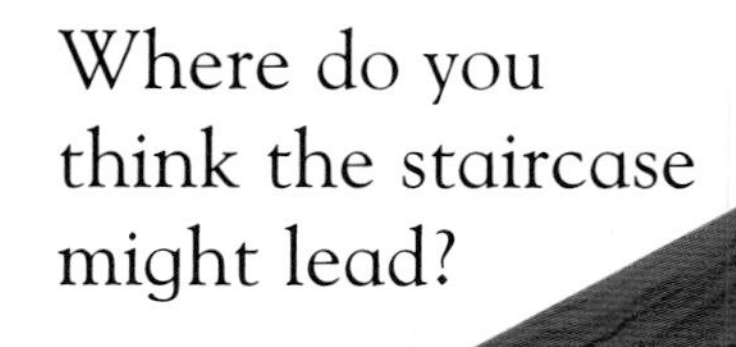

Where do you think the staircase might lead?

facts

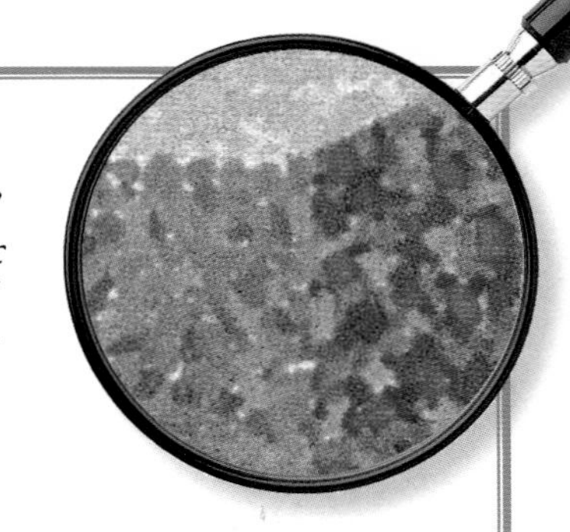

Look closer

Hockney has dabbed on several different colours of paint to achieve the speckled effect on the table.

Criss-cross pattern

This is a modern sculpture of a head. We can see two sides of the face at once. The artist Picasso developed this style.

The tulips are in a glass vase.

The side of the table farthest away from us is wider than the near side. Usually the farther away something is, the smaller it is.

Only the red outline of the chair is shown. The dark patch on the rug underneath looks like its shadow, but it is actually the shadow of a different type of chair.

The wooden staircase does not seem to go anywhere. It is surreal, like something from a dream that does not make sense.

Long ago people used to hang real curtains over their paintings to protect them. At first glance, this one could be real. This trick has been used by Dutch painters in the past.

Behind the scenes

Hockney painted this self-portrait in his London studio in 1977. He used oil paint on canvas.

ARTIST David Hockney

- He was born in England in 1937.
- Hockney likes to explore new ideas. As well as painting he has also worked in photography, printmaking, and stage design.
- He now lives in California.